# Mug Cakes

igloobooks

Published in 2015
by Igloo Books Ltd
Cottage Farm
Sywell
NN6 0BJ
www.igloobooks.com

Food photography and recipe development: PhotoCuisine UK
Front and back cover images © PhotoCuisine UK

HUN001 0615
2 4 6 8 10 9 7 5 3
ISBN 978-1-78440-402-4

Printed and manufactured in China

# Contents

# Classic

# Vanilla Mug Cake

**Makes:** 2  |  **Preparation Time:** 30 minutes  |  **Cooking Time:** 1 ½ minutes

## Ingredients

55 g / 2 oz / ¼ cup butter, softened

55 g / 2 oz / ¼ cup caster (superfine)
   sugar

1 large egg

½ tsp vanilla extract

55 g / 2 oz / ⅓ cup self-raising flour, sifted

### To decorate:

30 g / 1 oz / ½ cup butter, softened

75 g / 2 ½ oz / ¾ cup icing
   (confectioners') sugar, plus extra
   for dusting

½ tsp vanilla extract

½ vanilla pod, split lengthways

## Method

1. Beat the butter and sugar together in a mug until pale
   and smooth.

2. Break the egg into a second mug and add the vanilla
   extract. Beat gently with a fork, then gradually stir the
   egg into the butter mixture.

3. Fold in the flour and then spoon half of the mixture into
   the mug you used to beat the egg and level the tops.

4. Transfer the mugs to a microwave and cook on full
   power for 1 ½ minutes. Test the cakes by inserting
   a skewer into the centre – if it comes out clean, the
   cakes are ready. If not, return to the microwave for
   15 seconds and test again. Leave the cakes to cool
   completely.

5. Beat the butter, icing sugar and vanilla extract together
   until pale and well whipped, adding a few drops of hot
   water if the mixture is too stiff.

6. Spoon the buttercream into a piping bag fitted with
   a large star nozzle and pipe a big swirl on top of
   each cake.

7. Scrape the seeds out of the vanilla pod and dot them
   on top of the buttercream.

# Date and Walnut Mug Cake

**Makes:** 2  |  **Preparation Time:** 30 minutes  |  **Cooking Time:** 16 minutes

## Ingredients

55 g / 2 oz / ¼ cup butter, softened

55 g / 2 oz / ¼ cup caster (superfine) sugar

1 large egg

55 g / 2 oz / ⅓ cup self-raising flour, sifted

¼ tsp ground cinnamon

2 tsp walnuts, finely chopped

2–3 large dates, stoned and finely chopped

**To decorate:**

30 g / 1 oz / ½ cup butter, softened

75 g / 2 ½ oz / ¾ cup icing (confectioners') sugar, plus extra for dusting

½ tsp vanilla extract

2 large dates, stoned

4 walnut halves

## Method

1. Preheat the oven to 160°C (140°C fan) / 350F / gas 4.

2. Beat the butter and sugar together in an ovenproof mug until pale and smooth.

3. Break the egg into a second ovenproof mug. Beat gently with a fork, then gradually stir the egg into the butter mixture.

4. Fold in the flour, ground cinnamon, chopped walnuts and dates, then spoon half of the mixture into the mug you used to beat the egg and level the tops.

5. Transfer the mugs to a baking tray and cook in the centre of the oven for 16 minutes. Test the cakes by inserting a skewer into the centre – if it comes out clean, they're ready. If not, return to the oven for a couple of minutes and test again. Leave the cakes to cool completely.

6. Beat the butter, icing sugar and vanilla extract together until pale and smooth adding a few drops of hot water if the mixture is too stiff.

7. Spoon the buttercream into a piping bag fitted with a large plain nozzle and pipe a pillow on top of each cake. Top with a date and two walnut halves, then dust with icing sugar to serve.

# Chocolate Mug Cake

**Makes:** 1  |  **Preparation Time:** 5 Minutes  |  **Cooking Time:** 1 ½ minutes

## Ingredients

40 g / 1½ oz / ¼ cup self-raising flour

40 g / 1½ oz / ¼ cup caster
    (superfine) sugar

20 g / ¾ oz / ⅛ cup cocoa powder

1 medium egg

2 tbsp milk

2 tbsp vegetable oil

1 tbsp chocolate chips

1 tsp icing (confectioners') sugar

## Method

1. Mix the flour, sugar and cocoa in a large mug.
2. Add the egg and thoroughly mix.
3. Combine the milk and oil in another mug and add to the batter and stir.
4. Fold in the chocolate chips.
5. Place the mug in the centre of the microwave and cook for 1 ½ minutes on full power.
6. Check the cake by placing a skewer into the centre of the cake; it should come out clean when fully cooked.
7. Sprinkle with icing sugar and serve.

# Victoria Sponge Mug Cake

**Makes:** 1 | **Preparation Time:** 5 Minutes | **Cooking Time:** 1 ½ minutes

## Ingredients

30 g / 1 oz / ⅛ cup butter

30 g / 1 oz / ⅛ cup caster
(superfine) sugar

1 medium egg

30 g / 1 oz / ⅛ cup self-raising flour

1 tbsp milk

1 tsp vanilla extract

1 tbsp strawberry jam (jelly), sieved

**To decorate:**

1 tsp caster (superfine) sugar

fresh strawberries

## Method

1. Mix the butter and sugar in a large mug.

2. Add the egg and stir until well mixed.

3. Gradually stir in the flour and add the milk and vanilla extract; mix well.

4. Drop in the strawberry jam and allow to sink into the mixture without stirring.

5. Place the mug in the centre of the microwave and cook for 1 ½ minutes until well risen or until a skewer inserted in the centre comes out clean.

6. Sprinkle caster sugar on top and garnish with fresh strawberries.

# Coconut Mug Cake

---

**Makes:** 1  |  **Preparation Time:** 5 Minutes  |  **Cooking Time:** 1 ½ minutes

---

## Ingredients

30 g / 1 oz / ⅛ cup butter

30 g / 1 oz / ⅛ cup caster
(superfine) sugar

1 medium egg

30 g / 1 oz / ⅛ cup self-raising flour

1 tbsp milk

1 tbsp desiccated coconut

**To serve:**

1 scoop of coconut ice cream

1 tsp desiccated coconut

## Method

1. Mix the butter and sugar in a large mug.

2. Add the egg and stir until well mixed.

3. Gradually stir in the flour, then add the milk and mix well.

4. Fold in the coconut.

5. Place the mug in the centre of the microwave and cook for 1 ½ minutes until well risen or until a skewer inserted in the centre comes out clean.

6. Top with coconut ice cream, sprinkle with a little desiccated coconut and serve immediately.

# Coffee and Walnut Mug Cake

**Makes:** 2 | **Preparation Time:** 30 minutes | **Cooking Time:** 1 ½ minutes

## Ingredients

55 g / 2 oz / ¼ cup butter, softened

55 g / 2 oz / ¼ cup caster (superfine) sugar

1 large egg

55 g / 2 oz / ⅓ cup self-raising flour, sifted

1 tsp instant espresso powder or 1 tsp coffee essence

1 tbsp cocoa powder

1 tbsp walnuts, finely chopped

### To decorate:

30 g / 1 oz / ½ cup butter, softened

75 g / 2 ½ oz / ¾ cup icing (confectioners') sugar

½ tsp instant espresso powder or 1 tsp coffee essence

1 tbsp walnuts, finely chopped

4 chocolate coffee beans

## Method

1.  Beat the butter and sugar together in a mug until pale and smooth.

2.  Break the egg into a second mug and beat gently with a fork, then gradually stir the egg into the butter mixture.

3.  Fold in the flour, espresso powder / coffee essence and cocoa powder. Stir through the chopped walnut pieces. Spoon half of the mixture into the mug you used to beat the egg and level the tops.

4.  Transfer the mugs to a microwave and cook on full power for 1 ½ minutes. Test the cakes by inserting a skewer into the centre – if it comes out clean, they're ready. If not, return to the microwave for 15 seconds and test again. Leave the cakes to cool completely.

5.  Beat the butter, icing sugar and espresso powder / coffee essence together until pale and well whipped, adding a few drops of hot water if the mixture is too stiff.

6.  Use a piping bag with a large star nozzle to pipe buttercream onto the cakes in a large swirl, decorate with chopped walnuts and chocolate coffee beans.

# Carrot Mug Cake

**Makes:** 2  |  **Preparation Time:** 15 Minutes  |  **Cooking Time:** 4 Minutes

## Ingredients

60 g / 2 oz / ¼ cup self-raising flour

30 g / 1 oz / ⅛ cup brown sugar

a pinch of salt

¼ tsp ground cinnamon, plus extra for sprinkling

2 tbsp vegetable oil

1 medium egg

1 tbsp milk

30 g / 1 oz / ⅛ cup carrot, finely grated

**For the frosting:**

30 g / 1 oz / ⅛ cup cream cheese

30 g / 1 oz / ⅛ cup icing (confectioners') sugar

## Method

1. Mix the dry ingredients in a bowl.

2. Mix the wet ingredients in another bowl and add the carrot and stir until well mixed.

3. Combine the two mixtures and divide between two mugs.

4. Place one of the mugs in the centre of the microwave and cook for 2 minutes. Check the cake after 1 ½ minutes by placing a skewer in the centre of the mug. If the skewer comes out clean the cake is ready. Repeat with the second mug. Allow to cool.

5. To make the frosting, mix the cream cheese with the icing sugar.

6. Top the cooled carrot cakes with the frosting and dust with a little cinnamon before serving.

# Mini Fruit Mug Cake

**Makes:** 2  |  **Preparation Time:** 30 minutes  |  **Cooking Time:** 16 minutes

## Ingredients

55 g / 2 oz / ¼ cup butter, softened

55 g / 2 oz / ¼ cup dark muscovado sugar

1 large egg

1 tsp citrus peel, finely chopped

2 tsp raisins

55 g / 2 oz / ⅓ cup self-raising flour, sifted

¼ tsp ground mixed spice

¼ tsp ground cinnamon

**To decorate:**

6–8 tbsp caster (superfine) sugar

4–6 tbsp water

4 tbsp whole pistachios, shelled and unsalted

2 tbsp dried cranberries

16 hazelnuts (cobnuts), shelled

4 whole almonds

## Method

1. Preheat the oven to 160°C (140°C fan) / 350F / gas 4.

2. Beat the butter and sugar together in an ovenproof mug until pale and smooth.

3. Break the egg into a second ovenproof mug. Beat gently with a fork, then gradually stir the egg into the butter mixture.

4. Fold in the peel, raisins, flour and ground spices, mixing well to combine. Then spoon half of the mixture into the mug you used to beat the egg and level the tops.

5. Transfer the mugs to a baking tray and cook in the centre of the oven for 16 minutes. Test the cakes by inserting a skewer into the centre – if it comes out clean, they're ready. If not, return to the oven for a couple of minutes and test again. Leave the cakes to cool completely.

6. Mix the sugar with the water over a medium heat until it has dissolved into a thick syrup. Brush the syrup over the tops of the cooled cakes.

7. Arrange the nuts and dried fruit across the cakes and serve.

# Ginger Mug Cake

**Makes:** 1  |  **Preparation Time:** 5 minutes  |  **Cooking Time:** 1 ½ minutes

## Ingredients

30 g / 1 oz / ⅛ cup butter, softened

30 g / 1 oz / ⅛ cup caster (superfine) sugar

1 medium egg

30 g / 1 oz / ⅛ cup self-raising flour

½ tsp ground ginger

1 tbsp milk

1 tbsp ginger conserve

**To decorate:**

1 tbsp ginger conserve or candied ginger pieces

## Method

1. Mix the butter and sugar in a large mug.
2. Add the egg and stir until well mixed.
3. Gradually stir in the flour and ginger.
4. Add the milk and mix well.
5. Fold in the ginger conserve.
6. Place the mug in the centre of the microwave and cook for 1 ½ minutes until well risen or until a skewer inserted in the centre comes out clean.
7. Top with more ginger conserve or candied ginger to serve.

# Almond Mug Cake

**Makes:** 1 | **Preparation Time:** 5 Minutes | **Cooking Time:** 1 ½ minutes

## Ingredients

30 g / 1 oz / ⅛ cup butter, softened

30 g / 1 oz / 1 ⅛ cup caster (superfine) sugar

1 medium egg

20 g / ¾ oz / ⅛ cup self-raising flour

2 tbsp ground almonds

1 tbsp milk

**For the frosting:**

1 tbsp icing (confectioners') sugar

2 tsp water

1 tbsp almonds

1 tsp strawberry jam (jelly)

## Method

1. Mix the butter and sugar in a large mug.

2. Add the egg and stir until well mixed.

3. Gradually stir in the flour and ground almonds.

4. Add the milk and mix well.

5. Place the mug in the centre of the microwave and cook for 1 ½ minutes until well risen or until a skewer inserted in the centre comes out clean.

6. Place the icing sugar in a clean mug and gradually add the water and stir.

7. Pour the icing over the cake, decorate with whole almonds and the jam and serve.

# Maple and Pecan Mug Cake

**Makes:** 2  |  **Preparation Time:** 30 minutes  |  **Cooking Time:** 1 ½ minutes

## Ingredients

55 g / 2 oz / ¼ cup butter, softened

55 g / 2 oz / ¼ cup caster (superfine) sugar

1 large egg

2 tsp natural maple syrup

55 g / 2 oz / ⅓ cup self-raising flour, sifted

8 pecan nuts, finely chopped

### To decorate:

30 g / 1 oz / ½ cup butter, softened

75 g / 2 ½ oz / ¾ cup icing (confectioners') sugar, plus extra for dusting

2 tsp natural maple syrup

10 pecan nuts, finely chopped

## Method

1. Beat the butter and sugar together in a mug until pale and smooth.

2. Break the egg into a second mug and add the maple syrup. Beat gently with a fork, then gradually stir the egg into the butter mixture.

3. Fold in the flour and chopped pecan nuts, then spoon half of the mixture into the mug you used to beat the egg and level the tops.

4. Transfer the mugs to a microwave and cook on full power for 1 ½ minutes. Test the cakes by inserting a skewer into the centre – if it comes out clean, they're ready. If not, return to the microwave for 15 seconds and test again. Leave the cakes to cool completely.

5. Beat the butter, icing sugar and 1 tsp maple syrup together until pale and well whipped, adding a few drops of hot water if the mixture is too stiff.

6. Spread the buttercream onto each cake and level with a palette knife. Dot a few drops of maple syrup around the outsides.

7. Arrange the pecan nut quarters in a flower in the centre of each cake and dust with a little icing sugar.

# Cherry Mug Cake

**Makes:** 1  |  **Preparation Time:** 5 Minutes  |  **Cooking Time:** 1 ½ minutes

## Ingredients

30 g / 1 oz / ⅛ cup butter

30 g / 1 oz / ⅛ cup caster
(superfine) sugar

1 medium egg

30 g / 1 oz / ⅛ cup self-raising flour

1 tbsp milk

2 tbsp glacé cherries, halved

## Method

1.  Mix the butter and sugar in a large mug.

2.  Add the egg and stir until well mixed.

3.  Gradually stir in the flour, then add the milk
    and mix well.

4.  Fold in the cherries.

5.  Place the mug in the centre of the microwave
    and cook for 1 ½ minutes until well risen or until
    a skewer inserted in the centre comes out clean.

# Lemon Curd Mug Cake

---

**Makes:** 2  |  **Preparation Time:** 20 minutes  |  **Cooking Time:** 1 ½ minutes

---

## Ingredients

55 g / 2 oz / ¼ cup butter, softened

55 g / 2 oz / ¼ cup caster (superfine) sugar

1 lemon, zest finely grated

1 large egg

55 g / 2 oz / ⅓ cup self-raising flour, sifted

2 tbsp lemon curd

**To decorate:**

1 tsp lemon juice

55 g / 2 oz / ½ cup icing (confectioners') sugar

## Method

1. Beat the butter, sugar and lemon zest together in a mug until pale and smooth.

2. Break the egg into a second mug and beat gently with a fork, then gradually stir the egg into the butter mixture.

3. Fold in the flour, followed by the lemon curd, and then spoon half of the mixture into the mug you used to beat the egg.

4. Transfer the mugs to a microwave and cook on full power for 1 ½ minutes. Test the cakes by inserting a skewer into the centre – if it comes out clean, the cakes are ready. If not, return to the microwave for 15 seconds and test again.

5. Leave the cakes to cool for at least 10 minutes while you make the icing. Stir the lemon juice into the icing sugar a few drops at a time until thick but pourable. Drizzle the icing over the cakes and serve warm or at room temperature.

# White Chocolate Mug Cake

**Makes:** 2 | **Preparation Time:** 30 minutes | **Cooking Time:** 1 ½ minutes

## Ingredients

55 g / 2 oz / ¼ cup butter, softened

55 g / 2 oz / ¼ cup caster (superfine) sugar

1 large egg

55 g / 2 oz / ⅓ cup self-raising flour, sifted

1 tbsp white chocolate chunks

**To decorate:**

100 g / 3 ½ oz / ⅔ bar of white chocolate

2 white chocolate cigarillos

2 plain chocolate cigarillos

## Method

1.  Beat the butter and sugar together in a mug until pale and smooth.

2.  Break the egg into a second mug. Beat gently with a fork, then gradually stir the egg into the butter mixture.

3.  Fold in the flour followed by the white chocolate chunks, then spoon half of the mixture into the mug you used to beat the egg and level the tops.

4.  Transfer the mugs to a microwave and cook on full power for 1 ½ minutes. Test the cakes by inserting a skewer into the centre – if it comes out clean, they're ready. If not, return to the microwave for 15 seconds and test again. Leave the cakes to cool completely.

5.  Melt the white chocolate over a bain-marie, saving a couple of pieces for making shavings.

6.  Spread each cake with melted chocolate and allow to cool a little. As the chocolate begins to harden, stick a white and a dark chocolate cigarillo into each cake.

7.  After the melted chocolate has set, make some chocolate shavings with the reserved white chocolate by shaving with a sharp paring knife.

8.  Sprinkle the top of each cake with the chocolate shavings.

# Marzipan Mug Cake

**Makes:** 2　|　**Preparation Time:** 30 minutes　|　**Cooking Time:** 1 ½ minutes

## Ingredients

55 g / 2 oz / ¼ cup butter, softened

55 g / 2 oz / ¼ cup caster (superfine)
　　sugar

1 large egg

½ tsp almond extract

55 g / 2 oz / ⅓ cup self-raising flour,
　　sifted

1 tbsp marzipan, cut into small chunks

**To decorate:**

1 small block of marzipan

icing (confectioners') sugar for dusting

## Method

1.　Beat the butter and sugar together in a mug until pale and smooth.

2.　Break the egg into a second mug and add the almond extract. Beat gently with a fork, then gradually stir the egg into the butter mixture.

3.　Fold in the flour and marzipan chunks then spoon half of the mixture into the mug you used to beat the egg and level the tops.

4.　Transfer the mugs to a microwave and cook on full power for 1 ½ minutes. Test the cakes by inserting a skewer into the centre – if it comes out clean, they're ready. If not, return to the microwave for 15 seconds and test again. Leave the cakes to cool completely.

5.　Roll out the marzipan on a lightly dusted surface until it is approximately ½ cm (¼ in) thick, then cut out two circles to match the size of the mug tops. Top each cake with a marzipan circle.

6.　Roll the remaining marzipan into balls and toast for a few seconds with a kitchen blow torch until lightly browned. Arrange the balls around the mug tops.

7.　Dust with icing sugar and serve.

# Chocolate Chip Mug Cake

**Makes:** 1  |  **Preparation Time:** 5 Minutes  |  **Cooking Time:** 1 ½ minutes

## Ingredients

30 g / 1 oz / ⅛ cup butter, softened

30 g / 1 oz / ⅛ cup caster (superfine) sugar

1 medium egg

30 g / 1 oz / ⅛ cup self-raising flour

1 tbsp milk

1 tbsp large chocolate chips

2 tsp orange marmalade

## Method

1. Mix the butter and sugar in a large mug.

2. Add the egg and stir until well mixed.

3. Gradually stir in the flour, then add the milk and mix well.

4. Fold in the chocolate chips and marmalade, reserving a little of each for the top.

5. Place the mug in the centre of the microwave and cook for 1 ½ minutes until well risen or until a skewer inserted in the centre comes out clean. Allow to cool, then drizzle a little marmalade and sprinkle the chocolate chips onto the top.

# Lemon Drizzle Mug Cake

**Makes:** 1 | **Preparation Time:** 15 Minutes | **Cooking Time:** 12 ½ Minutes

## Ingredients

30 g / 1 oz / ⅛ cup butter

30 g / 1 oz / ⅛ cup caster (superfine) sugar

1 medium egg

30 g / 1 oz / ⅛ cup self-raising flour

1 tbsp milk

lemon slice to decorate

### For the syrup:

1 tbsp caster (superfine) sugar

1 tbsp boiling water

zest and juice of half a lemon

## Method

1. Preheat the oven to 180°C (160°C fan) / 425F / gas 4.

2. In a mug, combine 1 tbsp caster sugar with 1 tbsp boiling water.

3. Stir in half of the lemon juice and cook in the centre of the microwave for 30 seconds.

4. Allow to cool.

5. In a clean mug, mix the butter and sugar.

6. Add the egg and stir until well mixed.

7. Gradually stir in the flour, then add the milk and mix well.

8. Stir in the zest and remaining lemon juice.

9. Place the mug in the centre of the oven and cook for 10–12 minutes until well risen or until a skewer inserted in the centre comes out clean.

10. Pour the lemon syrup over the cake whilst it is still warm.

11. Decorate with a lemon slice and serve.

# Cinnamon and Raisin Mug Cake

**Makes:** 2 | **Preparation Time:** 20 minutes | **Cooking Time:** 1 ½ minutes

## Ingredients

55 g / 2 oz / ¼ cup butter, softened

55 g / 2 oz / ¼ cup caster (superfine) sugar

1 large egg

55 g / 2 oz / ⅓ cup self-raising flour, sifted

1 tsp ground cinnamon

1 tbsp raisins

1 tbsp cinnamon sugar

1 cinnamon stick, halved

## Method

1. Beat the butter and sugar together in a mug until pale and smooth.

2. Break the egg into a second mug and beat gently with a fork, then gradually stir the egg into the butter mixture.

3. Fold in the flour and ground cinnamon, followed by the raisins, then spoon half of the mixture into the mug used to beat the egg and level the tops.

4. Transfer the mugs to a microwave and cook on full power for 1 ½ minutes. Test the cakes by inserting a skewer into the centre – if it comes out clean, they're ready. If not, return to the microwave for 15 seconds and test again.

5. Sprinkle the top of the cakes with cinnamon sugar and brown them lightly under a hot grill. Serve warm or at room temperature, garnished with cinnamon stick halves.

# Chocolate Hazelnut Mug Cake

**Makes:** 2  |  **Preparation Time:** 30 minutes  |  **Cooking Time:** 1 ½ minutes

## Ingredients

55 g / 2 oz / ¼ cup butter, softened

55 g / 2 oz / ¼ cup caster (superfine) sugar

1 large egg

55 g / 2 oz / ⅓ cup self-raising flour, sifted

2 tbsp cocoa powder

1 tbsp hazelnuts (cobnuts), finely chopped

1 tbsp chocolate hazelnut (cobnut) spread

**To decorate:**

30 g / 1 oz / ½ cup butter, softened

75 g / 2 ½ oz / ¾ cup icing (confectioners') sugar

2 tsp cocoa powder, plus a little extra for sprinkling

1 tbsp hazelnuts (cobnuts), finely chopped

## Method

1. Beat the butter and sugar together in a mug until pale and smooth.

2. Break the egg into a second mug and beat gently with a fork, then gradually stir the egg into the butter mixture.

3. Fold in the flour and cocoa powder. Stir through the chopped hazelnut pieces and chocolate spread. Spoon half of the mixture into the mug used to beat the egg and level the tops.

4. Transfer the mugs to a microwave and cook on full power for 1 ½ minutes. Test the cakes by inserting a skewer into the centre – if it comes out clean, they're ready. If not, return to the microwave for 15 seconds and test again. Leave the cakes to cool completely.

5. Beat the butter, icing sugar and cocoa powder until smooth and well whipped, adding a few drops of hot water if the mixture is too stiff.

6. Use a piping bag with a large star nozzle to pipe buttercream onto the cakes in a large swirl. Decorate with chopped hazelnuts and dust with cocoa powder.

# Banana Mug Cake

**Makes:** 2 | **Preparation Time:** 20 minutes | **Cooking Time:** 16 minutes

## Ingredients

55 g / 2 oz / ¼ cup butter, softened

55 g / 2 oz / ¼ cup caster (superfine) sugar

1 large egg

½ tsp vanilla extract

55 g / 2 oz / ⅓ cup self-raising flour, sifted

1 large banana, lightly mashed

6–8 dried banana chips

**To decorate:**

icing (confectioners') sugar for dusting

## Method

1. Preheat the oven to 160°C (140°C fan) / 350F / gas 4.

2. Beat the butter and sugar together in an ovenproof mug until pale and smooth.

3. Break the egg into a second ovenproof mug and add the vanilla extract. Beat gently with a fork, then gradually stir the egg into the butter mixture.

4. Fold in the flour and the mashed banana, then spoon half of the mixture into the mug you used to beat the egg and level the tops.

5. Top the cakes with banana chips, laying them flat onto the surface of the mixture.

6. Transfer the mugs to a baking tray and cook in the centre of the oven for 16 minutes. Test the cakes by inserting a skewer into the centre – if it comes out clean, they're ready. If not, return to the oven for a couple of minutes and test again. Leave the cakes to cool a little and firm up.

7. Dust with icing sugar and serve warm with fresh cream.

# Fruity

# Strawberry Delight Mug Cake

**Makes:** 2  |  **Preparation Time:** 15 Minutes  |  **Cooking Time:** 3 Minutes

## Ingredients

50 g / 1 ¾ oz / ⅓ cup self-raising flour

a pinch of salt

3 egg whites

¼ tsp cream of tartar

65 g / 2 ⅓ oz / ⅓ cup caster (superfine) sugar

strawberries for garnish

## Method

1. Sieve the self-raising flour and salt together.

2. Using an electric whisk, whisk the egg whites in a clean bowl until foamy.

3. Add the cream of tartar and whisk for 1 minute.

4. Gradually add the sugar whilst whisking until all the sugar is incorporated and stiff peaks form.

5. Using a spatula, fold in the flour and salt, a little at a time, until well mixed and a smooth batter is formed.

6. Divide the mixture between two large mugs.

7. Place one of the mugs in the centre of the microwave and cook for 1 ½ minutes at 60% power. Check the cake at 30 second intervals; a skewer should come out clean.

8. Place the second mug in the microwave and cook as before.

9. Garnish with fresh strawberries.

# Chocolate Orange Mug Cake

**Makes:** 1 | **Preparation Time:** 5 Minutes | **Cooking Time:** 1 ½ minutes

## Ingredients

40 g / 1 ½ oz / ¼ cup self-raising flour

40 g / 1 ½ oz / ¼ cup caster (superfine) sugar

20 g / ¾ oz / ⅛ cup cocoa powder

1 medium egg

2 tbsp milk

2 tbsp vegetable oil

1 tbsp chocolate chips

zest of ½ small orange, reserving some as garnish

## Method

1. Mix the flour, sugar and cocoa in a large mug.

2. Add the egg and thoroughly mix.

3. Combine the milk and oil in another mug, then add to the batter and stir.

4. Fold in the chocolate chips and the orange zest.

5. Place the mug in the centre of the microwave and cook for 1 ½ minutes on full power.

6. Check the cake by placing a skewer into the centre of the cake, it should come out clean when fully cooked.

7. Garnish with the remaining zest and serve.

# Apple Crumble Mug Cake

**Makes:** 2  |  **Preparation Time:** 30 minutes  |  **Cooking Time:** 1 ½ minutes

## Ingredients

55 g / 2 oz / ¼ cup butter, softened

55 g / 2 oz / ¼ cup caster (superfine) sugar

1 large egg

55 g / 2 oz / ⅓ cup self-raising flour, sifted

½ tsp ground cinnamon

1 small apple, peeled, cored and diced, 4 slices reserved to garnish

### For the crumble:

2 tbsp butter, diced

4 tbsp plain (all-purpose) flour

2 tbsp soft light brown sugar

## Method

1. Beat the butter and sugar together in a mug until pale and smooth.

2. Break the egg into a second mug and beat gently with a fork, then gradually stir the egg into the butter mixture.

3. Fold in the flour and ground cinnamon, followed by the apple, then spoon half of the mixture into the mug you used to beat the egg and level the tops.

4. To make the crumble topping, rub the butter into the flour, then stir in the sugar. Sprinkle it over the cake mixture in the mugs.

5. Transfer the mugs to a microwave and cook on full power for 1 ½ minutes. Test the cakes by inserting a skewer into the centre – if it comes out clean, they're ready. If not, return to the microwave for 15 seconds and test again.

6. Brown the crumble lightly under a hot grill and serve warm or at room temperature, topped with apple slices.

# Apple and Berry Mug Cake

**Makes:** 1 | **Preparation Time:** 15 Minutes | **Cooking Time:** 3 ½ Minutes

## Ingredients

30 g / 1 oz / ⅛ cup butter, softened

30 g / 1 oz / ⅛ cup caster (superfine)
  sugar

1 medium egg

30 g / 1 oz / ⅛ cup self-raising flour

1 tbsp milk

**For the compote:**

½ apple, finely cubed

2 large strawberries, diced

1 small handful of blackberries

1 tbsp caster (superfine) sugar

## Method

1. In a microwaveable bowl, place the apple, strawberries and blackberries (reserving a few for garnish) and sugar and mix well.

2. Cook in the microwave for 2 minutes, stir and set aside to cool.

3. Mix the butter and sugar in a large mug.

4. Add the egg and stir until well mixed.

5. Gradually stir in the flour, then add the milk and mix well.

6. Stir in half of the apple and berry compote.

7. Place the mug in the centre of the microwave and cook for 1 ½ minutes until well risen or until a skewer inserted in the centre comes out clean.

8. Place the remaining fruit compote on top to serve.

# Citrus Mug Cake

**Makes:** 2 | **Preparation Time:** 20 minutes | **Cooking Time:** 1 ½ minutes

## Ingredients

55 g / 2 oz / ¼ cup butter, softened

55 g / 2 oz / ¼ cup caster (superfine) sugar

1 large egg

1 tsp orange extract

55 g / 2 oz / ⅓ cup self-raising flour, sifted

½ lemon, zested

½ lime, zested

### To decorate:

30 g / 1 oz / ½ cup butter, softened

75 g / 2 ½ oz / ¾ cup icing (confectioners') sugar, plus extra for dusting

1 tsp orange extract

1 tsp green sugar balls

## Method

1. Beat the butter and sugar together in a mug until pale and smooth.

2. Break the egg into a second mug and add the orange extract. Beat gently with a fork, then gradually stir the egg into the butter mixture.

3. Fold in the flour and stir through the lemon and lime zest, then spoon half of the mixture into the mug you used to beat the egg and level the tops.

4. Transfer the mugs to a microwave and cook on full power for 1 ½ minutes. Test the cakes by inserting a skewer into the centre – if it comes out clean, they're ready. If not, return to the microwave for 15 seconds and test again. Leave the cakes to cool completely.

5. Beat the butter, icing sugar and orange extract together until pale and creamy, adding a few drops of hot water if the mixture is too stiff.

6. Spoon the buttercream into a piping bag fitted with a medium plain nozzle and pipe a spiral swirl on top of each cake.

7. Decorate with the green sugar balls.

# Very Berry Mug Cake

**Makes:** 2　|　**Preparation Time:** 20 minutes　|　**Cooking Time:** 1 ½ minutes

## Ingredients

55 g / 2 oz / ¼ cup butter, softened

55 g / 2 oz / ¼ cup caster (superfine) sugar

1 large egg

55 g / 2 oz / ⅓ cup self-raising flour, sifted

3 tbsp mixed berries, defrosted if frozen

**To decorate:**

30 g / 1 oz / ½ cup butter, softened

75 g / 2 ½ oz / ¾ cup icing (confectioners') sugar, plus extra for dusting

½ tsp vanilla extract

2 tbsp mixed berries, defrosted if frozen

## Method

1. Beat the butter and sugar together in a mug until pale and smooth.

2. Break the egg into a second mug and beat gently with a fork, then gradually stir the egg into the butter mixture.

3. Fold in the flour, followed by the berries, then spoon half of the mixture into the mug you used to beat the egg and level the tops.

4. Transfer the mugs to a microwave and cook on full power for 1 ½ minutes. Test the cakes by inserting a skewer into the centre – if it comes out clean, they're ready. If not, return to the microwave for 15 seconds and test again. Leave the cakes to cool completely.

5. Beat the butter, icing sugar and vanilla extract together until pale and well whipped, adding a few drops of hot water if the mixture is too stiff.

6. Spoon the buttercream into a piping bag fitted with a large star nozzle and pipe a big ring on top of each cake. Fill the centre of the rings with berries and serve immediately.

# Orange and Cranberry Mug Cake

**Makes:** 1   |   **Preparation Time:** 10 Minutes   |   **Cooking Time:** 1 ½ minutes

## Ingredients

30 g / 1 oz / ⅛ cup butter, softened

30 g / 1 oz / ⅛ cup caster
  (superfine) sugar

1 medium egg

30 g / 1 oz / ⅛ cup self-raising flour

1 tbsp milk

1 tbsp dried cranberries soaked in
  1 tsp orange liqueur

zest of ½ orange

1 tbsp orange juice

**To decorate:**

1 tbsp dried cranberries soaked in
  1 tsp orange liqueur

1 segment of satsuma

## Method

1. Mix the butter and sugar in a large mug.

2. Add the egg and stir until well mixed.

3. Gradually stir in the flour, then add the milk
   and mix well.

4. Fold in the soaked cranberries, orange zest
   and juice.

5. Place the mug in the centre of the microwave
   and cook for 1 ½ minutes until well risen or
   until a skewer inserted in the centre comes
   out clean.

6. Top with more soaked cranberries and the
   satsuma segment.

# Raspberry Pavlova Mug Cake

**Makes:** 2 | **Preparation Time:** 30 minutes | **Cooking Time:** 1 ½ minutes

## Ingredients

55 g / 2 oz / ¼ cup butter, softened

55 g / 2 oz / ¼ cup caster (superfine) sugar

1 large egg

55 g / 2 oz / ⅓ cup self-raising flour, sifted

2 tbsp fresh raspberries, chopped

**To decorate:**

250 ml / 9 fl. oz / 1 cup fresh whipping cream

6 fresh raspberries

2 mini meringues

## Method

1. Beat the butter and sugar together in a mug until pale and glossy.

2. Break the egg into a second mug. Beat gently with a fork, then gradually stir the egg into the butter mixture.

3. Fold in the flour and the chopped fresh raspberries, then spoon half of the mixture into the mug you used to beat the egg and level the tops.

4. Transfer the mugs to a microwave and cook on full power for 1 ½ minutes. Test the cakes by inserting a skewer into the centre – if it comes out clean, they're ready. If not, return to the microwave for 15 seconds and test again. Leave the cakes to cool completely.

5. Whip the cream with an electric whisk until it is light and fluffy, and holds its shape. It should be of piping consistency.

6. Spoon the cream into a piping bag fitted with a small plain nozzle and pipe teardrops around the outsides of the cakes.

7. Arrange the fresh raspberries in the centre and top with a mini meringue before serving.

# Summer Fruit Mug Cake

**Makes:** 1  |  **Preparation Time:** 5 Minutes  |  **Cooking Time:** 2 Minutes

## Ingredients

30 g / 1 oz / ⅛ cup butter, softened

30 g / 1 oz / ⅛ cup caster
   (superfine) sugar

1 medium egg

30 g / 1 oz / ⅛ cup self-raising flour

1 tbsp milk

1 tbsp frozen mixed berries (defrosted)

**For the topping:**

1 tbsp frozen mixed berries (defrosted)

1 tbsp strawberry jam (jelly)

## Method

1. Mix the butter and sugar in a large mug.

2. Add the egg and stir until well mixed.

3. Gradually stir in the flour, then add the milk and mix well.

4. Fold in the mixed berries.

5. Place the mug in the centre of the microwave and cook for 1 ½ minutes until well risen or until a skewer inserted in the centre comes out clean. Allow to cool.

6. In a separate mug combine the frozen berries and jam, then cook for 30 seconds.

7. Spoon the cooked berries onto the cake and serve.

# Pineapple and Banana Mug Cake

---

**Makes:** 2 | **Preparation Time:** 20 minutes | **Cooking Time:** 1 ½ minutes

---

## Ingredients

55 g / 2 oz / ¼ cup butter, softened

55 g / 2 oz / ¼ cup caster (superfine) sugar

1 large egg

½ tsp vanilla extract

½ fresh banana, roughly mashed

2 tbsp canned pineapple chunks, drained and finely chopped

55 g / 2 oz / ⅓ cup self-raising flour, sifted

### To decorate:

30 g / 1 oz / ½ cup butter, softened

75 g / 2 ½ oz / ¾ cup icing (confectioners') sugar, plus extra for dusting

½ tsp vanilla extract

6 pieces of dried or candied pineapple

## Method

1. Beat the butter and sugar together in a mug until pale and smooth.

2. Break the egg into a second mug and add the vanilla extract. Beat gently with a fork, then gradually stir the egg into the butter mixture. Mix through the banana and pineapple pieces.

3. Fold in the flour, then spoon half of the mixture into the mug you used to beat the egg and level the tops.

4. Transfer the mugs to a microwave and cook on full power for 1 ½ minutes. Test the cakes by inserting a skewer into the centre – if it comes out clean, they're ready. If not, return to the microwave for 15 seconds and test again. Leave the cakes to cool completely.

5. Beat the butter, icing sugar and vanilla extract together until pale and creamy, adding a few drops of hot water if the mixture is too stiff.

6. Spoon the buttercream into a piping bag fitted with a small plain nozzle and pipe teardrops around top of each cake.

7. Top each cake with a few pieces of dried or candied pineapple and dust with icing sugar to serve.

# Honey and Lemon Mug Cake

---

**Makes:** 2  |  **Preparation Time:** 30 minutes  |  **Cooking Time:** 1 ½ minutes

---

## Ingredients

55 g / 2 oz / ¼ cup butter, softened

55 g / 2 oz / ¼ cup caster (superfine) sugar

1 large egg

2 tbsp runny honey

2 tbsp lemon juice

55 g / 2 oz / ⅓ cup self-raising flour, sifted

½ unwaxed lemon, zested

**To decorate:**

30 g / 1 oz / ½ cup butter, softened

75 g / 2 ½ oz / ¾ cup icing (confectioners') sugar

2 tbsp runny honey  plus a little extra for drizzling

½ tsp lemon extract

2 thick slices of unwaxed lemon

## Method

1. Beat the butter and sugar together in a mug until pale and silky.

2. Break the egg into a second mug and add the runny honey and lemon juice. Beat gently with a fork, then gradually stir the egg into the butter mixture.

3. Fold in the flour and lemon zest and then spoon half of the mixture into the mug you used to beat the egg and level the tops.

4. Transfer the mugs to a microwave and cook on full power for 1 ½ minutes. Test the cakes by inserting a skewer into the centre – if it comes out clean, they're ready. If not, return to the microwave for 20 seconds and test again. Leave the cakes to cool completely.

5. Beat the butter, icing sugar, honey and lemon extract together until pale and well whipped, adding a few drops of hot water if the mixture is too stiff.

6. Spread the buttercream evenly on top of the cakes with a palette knife.

7. Top each cake with a slice of lemon drizzled with a little honey and serve.

# Coconut Lime Mug Cake

**Makes:** 2  |  **Preparation Time:** 30 minutes  |  **Cooking Time:** 1 ½ minutes

## Ingredients

55 g / 2 oz / ¼ cup butter, softened

55 g / 2 oz / ¼ cup caster (superfine) sugar

1 large egg

½ tsp lime extract

55 g / 2 oz / ⅓ cup self-raising flour, sifted

4 tsp desiccated coconut

½ lime, zested

**To decorate:**

30 g / 1 oz / ½ cup butter, softened

75 g / 2 ½ oz / ¾ cup icing (confectioners') sugar

½ tsp lime extract

2 tsp dried coconut pieces

½ lime, zested

## Method

1. Beat the butter and sugar together in a mug until pale and smooth.

2. Break the egg into a second mug and add the lime extract. Beat gently with a fork, then gradually stir the egg into the butter mixture.

3. Fold in the flour and stir through the desiccated coconut and lime zest, then spoon half of the mixture into the mug you used to beat the egg and level the tops.

4. Transfer the mugs to a microwave and cook on full power for 1 ½ minutes. Test the cakes by inserting a skewer into the centre – if it comes out clean, they're ready. If not, return to the microwave for 15 seconds and test again. Leave the cakes to cool completely.

5. Beat the butter, icing sugar and lime extract together until pale and creamy, adding a few drops of hot water if the mixture is too stiff.

6. Spoon the buttercream onto the top of each cake and smooth into a dome with the back of a spoon.

7. Top with the dried coconut pieces and sprinkle with the lime zest before serving.

Fruity

# Raspberry Swirl Mug Cake

**Makes:** 1 | **Preparation Time:** 7 Minutes | **Cooking Time:** 1 ½ minutes

## Ingredients

30 g / 1 oz / ⅛ cup butter, softened

30 g / 1 oz / ⅛ cup caster
(superfine) sugar

1 medium egg

30 g / 1 oz / ⅛ cup self-raising flour

1 tbsp milk

1 tbsp freeze-dried raspberry pieces

**For the frosting:**

10 g / ⅓ oz / ⅛ cup butter, softened

20 g / ¾ oz / ¼ cup icing (confectioners')
sugar

1 tbsp raspberry jam (jelly), sieved

1 tsp freeze-dried raspberry pieces

## Method

1. Mix the butter and sugar in a large mug.

2. Add the egg and stir until well mixed.

3. Gradually stir in the flour, then add the milk and
   mix well.

4. Stir in the raspberries.

5. Place the mug in the centre of the microwave
   and cook for 1 ½ minutes until well risen or until
   a skewer inserted in the centre comes out clean.

6. To make the frosting, combine the butter and icing
   sugar and mix well.

7. Gently fold in the raspberry jam, to create a
   swirl effect.

8. Pipe or spoon onto the cooled cake and sprinkle
   with more freeze-dried raspberry pieces.

# Black Cherry Mug Cake

**Makes:** 2 | **Preparation Time:** 30 minutes | **Cooking Time:** 1 ½ minutes

## Ingredients

55 g / 2 oz / ¼ cup butter, softened

55 g / 2 oz / ¼ cup caster (superfine) sugar

1 large egg

55 g / 2 oz / ⅓ cup self-raising flour, sifted

3 tbsp chunky black cherry pie filling

**To decorate:**

30 g / 1 oz / ½ cup butter, softened

75 g / 2 ½ oz / ¾ cup icing (confectioners') sugar

½ tsp vanilla extract

2 tbsp black cherry pie filling or jam (jelly)

## Method

1. Beat the butter and sugar together in a mug until pale and smooth.

2. Break the egg into a second mug and beat gently with a fork, then gradually stir the egg into the butter mixture.

3. Fold in the flour and swirl in the cherry pie filling, then spoon half of the mixture into the mug you used to beat the egg and level the tops.

4. Transfer the mugs to a microwave and cook on full power for 1 ½ minutes. Test the cakes by inserting a skewer into the centre – if it comes out clean, they're ready. If not, return to the microwave for 15 seconds and test again. Leave the cakes to cool.

5. Beat the butter, icing sugar and vanilla extract together until pale and well whipped, adding a few drops of hot water if the mixture is too stiff.

6. Spoon the buttercream into a piping bag fitted with a small plain nozzle and pipe some teardrops around one side of each cake.

7. Spoon a little jam or pie filling onto the top of the cake and serve.

# Pear and Fig Mug Cake

**Makes:** 2  |  **Preparation Time:** 30 minutes  |  **Cooking Time:** 16 minutes

## Ingredients

55 g / 2 oz / ¼ cup butter, softened

55 g / 2 oz / ¼ cup caster (superfine) sugar

1 large egg

1 ½ tsp sirop de figue

55 g / 2 oz / ⅓ cup self-raising flour, sifted

2 dried figs, finely chopped

2 canned pear halves, finely diced

**To decorate:**

icing (confectioners') sugar for dusting

## Method

1.  Preheat the oven to 160°C (140°C fan) / 350F / gas 4.

2.  Beat the butter and sugar together in an ovenproof mug until pale and smooth.

3.  Break the egg into a second ovenproof mug and add the sirop de figue. Beat gently with a fork, then gradually stir the egg into the butter mixture.

4.  Fold in the flour, chopped figs and diced pears. Next, spoon half of the mixture into the mug you used to beat the egg and level the tops by tapping once on a work surface.

5.  Transfer the mugs to a baking tray and cook in the centre of the oven for 16 minutes. Test the cakes by inserting a skewer into the centre – if it comes out clean, they're ready. If not, return to the oven for a couple of minutes and test again. Leave the cakes to cool a little.

6.  Dust each cake with a little icing sugar before serving warm. Vanilla ice cream makes an ideal accompaniment to these cakes.

# Apricot Mug Cake

**Makes:** 2  |  **Preparation Time:** 30 minutes  |  **Cooking Time:** 1 ½ minutes

## Ingredients

55 g / 2 oz / ¼ cup butter, softened

55 g / 2 oz / ¼ cup caster (superfine) sugar

1 large egg

55 g / 2 oz / ⅓ cup self-raising flour, sifted

4 canned apricot halves, finely diced

1 tbsp apricot jam (jelly)

**To decorate:**

30 g / 1 oz / ½ cup butter, softened

75 g / 2 ½ oz / ¾ cup icing (confectioners') sugar, plus extra for dusting

½ tsp vanilla extract

6 canned apricot halves

## Method

1. Beat the butter and sugar together in a mug until pale and smooth.

2. Break the egg into a second mug and beat gently with a fork, then gradually stir the egg into the butter mixture.

3. Fold in the flour, followed by the apricot pieces and jam, then spoon half of the mixture into the mug you used to beat the egg and level the tops.

4. Transfer the mugs to a microwave and cook on full power for 1 ½ minutes. Test the cakes by inserting a skewer into the centre – if it comes out clean, they're ready. If not, return to the microwave for 15 seconds and test again. Leave the cakes to cool completely.

5. Beat the butter and icing sugar and vanilla extract together until pale and creamy.

6. Spoon the buttercream into a piping bag fitted with a large plain nozzle and pipe a ring round the edge of each cake.

7. Fill the centre of each buttercream ring with the apricot halves.

# Blackberry Cheesecake Mug Cake

**Makes:** 2  |  **Preparation Time:** 30 minutes  |  **Cooking Time:** 1 ½ minutes

## Ingredients

55 g / 2 oz / ¼ cup butter, softened

55 g / 2 oz / ¼ cup caster (superfine) sugar

1 large egg

55 g / 2 oz / ⅓ cup self-raising flour, sifted

2 tbsp fresh blackberries, chopped

To decorate:

250 ml / 9 fl. oz / 1 cup fresh whipping cream

2 tbsp icing (confectioners') sugar, plus extra for dusting

2 tbsp cream cheese

4–6 fresh blackberries

## Method

1. Beat the butter and sugar together in a mug until pale and shiny.

2. Break the egg into a second mug. Beat gently with a fork, then gradually stir the egg into the butter mixture.

3. Fold in the flour and the chopped blackberries, then spoon half of the mixture into the mug you used to beat the egg and level the tops.

4. Transfer the mugs to a microwave and cook on full power for 1 ½ minutes. Test the cakes by inserting a skewer into the centre – if it comes out clean, they're ready. If not, return to the microwave for 15 seconds and test again. Leave the cakes to cool completely.

5. Whip the cream with an electric whisk until it holds its shape. It should be of piping consistency.

6. Mix the icing sugar with the cream cheese until combined. Spread a layer of the sweetened cheese onto the cake tops of the cakes and smooth with a palette knife.

7. Spoon the cream into a piping bag fitted with a medium plain nozzle and pipe a generous pillow of fresh cream on top of the cheese layer.

8. Arrange the fresh blackberries in the centre and dust with icing sugar before serving.

# Indulgent

# Rich Chocolate Chip Mug Cake

**Makes:** 2 | **Preparation Time:** 15 minutes | **Cooking Time:** 1 ½ minutes

## Ingredients

55 g / 2 oz / ¼ cup butter, softened

55 g / 2 oz / ¼ cup caster (superfine) sugar

1 large egg

55 g / 2 oz / ⅓ cup self-raising flour, sifted

1 tbsp cocoa powder

3 tbsp milk chocolate chunks

icing (confectioners') sugar for dusting

## Method

1. Beat the butter and sugar together in a mug until pale and smooth.

2. Break the egg into a second mug and beat gently with a fork, then gradually stir the egg into the butter mixture.

3. Fold in the flour and cocoa powder, followed by the chocolate chunks, and then spoon half of the mixture into the mug you used to beat the egg and level the tops.

4. Transfer the mugs to a microwave and cook on full power for 1 ½ minutes. Test the cakes by inserting a skewer into the centre – if it comes out clean, the cakes are ready. If not, return to the microwave for 15 seconds and test again.

5. Leave the cakes to stand for 5 minutes, and then dust lightly with icing sugar and serve.

# Salted Caramel Mug Cake

**Makes:** 1 | **Preparation Time:** 5 Minutes | **Cooking Time:** 5 Minutes

## Ingredients

30 g / 1 oz / ⅛ cup butter

30 g / 1 oz / ⅛ cup caster (superfine) sugar

1 tsp vanilla extract

1 medium egg

30 g / 1 oz / ⅛ cup self-raising flour

1 tbsp milk

**For the caramel sauce:**

2 tbsp caster (superfine) sugar

1 tbsp boiling water

2 tsp salted butter

1 tbsp double (heavy) cream

a pinch of salt

## Method

1. Mix the butter, sugar and vanilla extract in a large mug.

2. Add the egg and stir until well mixed.

3. Gradually stir in the flour, then add the milk and mix well.

4. Place the mug in the centre of the microwave and cook for 1 ½ minutes until well risen or until a skewer inserted in the centre comes out clean.

5. For the caramel, combine the sugar and water in a clean mug.

6. Cook in the microwave for up to 3 minutes or until the sugar has started to caramelise and turn golden brown.

7. Immediately add the butter, cream and salt and then stir carefully but quickly to combine.

8. Pour over the sponge and serve.

# Malted Chocolate Mug Cake

**Makes:** 2 | **Preparation Time:** 30 minutes | **Cooking Time:** 16 minutes

## Ingredients

55 g / 2 oz / ¼ cup butter, softened

55 g / 2 oz / ¼ cup caster (superfine) sugar

1 large egg

55 g / 2 oz / ⅓ cup self-raising flour, sifted

1 tbsp cocoa powder

### To decorate:

4 tbsp chocolate spread

1 small packet of malted chocolate balls

1 tbsp cocoa powder plus extra for dusting

## Method

1. Preheat the oven to 160°C (140°C fan) / 350F / gas 4.

2. Beat the butter and sugar together in an ovenproof mug until pale and smooth.

3. Break the egg into a second ovenproof mug and beat gently with a fork, then gradually stir the egg into the butter mixture.

4. Fold in the flour and cocoa powder and mix well to combine. Spoon half of the mixture into the mug you used to beat the egg and level the tops.

5. Transfer the mugs to a baking tray and cook in the centre of the oven for 16 minutes. Test the cakes by inserting a skewer into the centre – if it comes out clean, they're ready. If not, return to the oven for a couple of minutes and test again. Leave the cakes to cool completely.

6. Spread the tops of the cakes with the chocolate spread.

7. Cover the tops with malted chocolate balls and dust with cocoa powder.

# Vanilla Fudge Mug Cake

**Makes:** 1 | **Preparation Time:** 5 Minutes | **Cooking Time:** 1 ½ minutes

## Ingredients

30 g / 1 oz / ⅛ cup butter, softened

30 g / 1 oz / ⅛ cup caster
   (superfine) sugar

1 medium egg

30 g / 1 oz / ⅛ cup self-raising flour

1 tbsp milk

1 tsp vanilla extract

2 tbsp fudge pieces

## Method

1. Mix the butter and sugar in a large mug.

2. Add the egg and stir until well mixed.

3. Gradually stir in the flour and add the milk
   and vanilla extract; mix well.

4. Fold in the fudge pieces.

5. Place the mug in the centre of the microwave
   and cook for 1 ½ minutes until well risen or until
   a skewer inserted in the centre comes out clean.

# Caffè Latte Mug Cake

**Makes:** 1  |  **Preparation Time:** 30 minutes  |  **Cooking Time:** 1 ½ minutes

## Ingredients

55 g / 2 oz / ¼ cup butter, softened

55 g / 2 oz / ¼ cup caster (superfine) sugar

1 large egg

2 tbsp sweetened coffee and chicory essence

55 g / 2 oz / ⅓ cup self-raising flour, sifted

### To decorate:

30 g / 1 oz / ½ cup butter, softened

½ tsp vanilla extract

75 g / 2 ½ oz / ¾ cup icing (confectioners') sugar

cocoa powder for sprinkling

2 chocolate-covered coffee beans

## Method

1. Beat the butter and sugar together in a mug until pale and silky.

2. Break the egg into a second mug and beat gently with a fork and combine with the coffee essence, then gradually stir the egg mixture into the butter mixture.

3. Fold in the flour and combine well. Spoon half of the mixture into the mug you used to beat the egg and level the tops.

4. Transfer the mugs to a microwave and cook on full power for 1 ½ minutes. Test the cakes by inserting a skewer into the centre – if it comes out clean, they're ready. If not, return to the microwave for 15 seconds and test again. Leave the cakes to cool completely.

5. Beat the butter, vanilla extract and icing sugar until pale and well whipped, adding a few drops of hot water if the mixture is too stiff.

6. Put the buttercream into a piping bag with a small plain nozzle and pipe teardrops onto the tops of each cake.

7. Sprinkle with a little cocoa powder and top with a chocolate-covered coffee bean.

# Cookies and Cream Mug Cake

**Makes:** 2 | **Preparation Time:** 30 minutes | **Cooking Time:** 1 ½ minutes

## Ingredients

55 g / 2 oz / ¼ cup butter, softened

55 g / 2 oz / ¼ cup caster (superfine) sugar

1 large egg

55 g / 2 oz / ⅓ cup self-raising flour, sifted

4 mini chocolate cookies, roughly chopped

**To decorate:**

30 g / 1 oz / ½ cup butter, softened

75 g / 2 ½ oz / ¾ cup icing (confectioners') sugar, plus extra for dusting

½ tsp vanilla extract

4 mini chocolate cookies

## Method

1. Beat the butter and sugar together in a mug until pale and smooth.

2. Break the egg into a second mug and beat gently with a fork, then gradually stir the egg into the butter mixture.

3. Fold in the flour, followed by the chopped cookies, and then spoon half of the mixture into the mug you used to beat the egg and level the tops.

4. Transfer the mugs to a microwave and cook on full power for 1 ½ minutes. Test the cakes by inserting a skewer into the centre – if it comes out clean, the cakes are ready. If not, return to the microwave for 15 seconds and test again. Leave the cakes to cool completely.

5. Beat the butter, icing sugar and vanilla extract together until pale and well whipped, adding a few drops of hot water if the mixture is too stiff.

6. Spoon the buttercream into a piping bag and pipe a big swirl on top of each cake.

7. Crumble two of the cookies into crumbs and sprinkle on top before garnishing each cake with a whole cookie.

# Sticky Toffee Mug Cake

**Makes:** 4 | **Preparation Time:** 15 Minutes | **Cooking Time:** 8–10 Minutes

## Ingredients

90 g / 3 ¼ oz / ½ cup finely chopped, pitted dates, plus 4 whole dates to serve

90 ml / 3 fl. oz / ⅓ cup boiling water

40 g / 1 ½ oz / ¼ cup butter, softened

75 g / 2 ½ oz / ½ cup dark brown sugar

1 medium egg

90 g / 3 ¼ oz / ½ cup self-raising flour

½ tsp bicarbonate of (baking) soda

**For the toffee sauce:**

2 tbsp dark brown sugar

2 tsp boiling water

1 tbsp double (heavy) cream

## Method

1. Soak the finely-chopped dates in the boiling water for 5 minutes.
2. Cook in the microwave for 2 minutes.
3. Liquidise or mash the dates with a fork and set aside.
4. In a bowl mix the butter and the sugar and whisk until light and fluffy.
5. Add the egg and whisk further.
6. Add the flour and bicarbonate of soda.
7. Gently fold in the date mixture.
8. Divide between the 4 mugs.
9. Place each mug in the centre of the microwave and cook for 1 ½ minutes or until a skewer inserted in the centre comes out clean.
10. To make the toffee sauce, stir the sugar and water in another mug and cook for 3 minutes.
11. Stir in the cream and pour over the cooked cakes.

# Pistachio Mug Cake

**Makes:** 1 | **Preparation Time:** 5 Minutes | **Cooking Time:** 1 ½ minutes

## Ingredients

30 g / 1 oz / ⅛ cup butter, softened

30 g / 1 oz / ⅛ cup caster
(superfine) sugar

1 tsp green food dye

1 medium egg

20 g / ¾ oz / ⅛ cup self-raising flour

2 tbsp ground pistachios

1 tbsp milk

**To decorate:**

icing (confectioners') sugar to sprinkle

1 whole pistachio nut

## Method

1. Mix the butter, sugar and food dye in a large mug.

2. Add the egg and stir until well mixed.

3. Gradually stir in the flour and ground pistachios.

4. Add the milk, then mix well.

5. Place the mug in the centre of the microwave and cook for 1 ½ minutes until well risen or until a skewer inserted in the centre comes out clean.

6. Dust with icing sugar and top with the whole pistachio nut.

# Marshmallow Surprise Mug Cake

**Makes:** 2  |  **Preparation Time:** 30 minutes  |  **Cooking Time:** 1 ½ minutes

## Ingredients

55 g / 2 oz / ¼ cup butter, softened

55 g / 2 oz / ¼ cup caster (superfine) sugar

1 large egg

½ tsp vanilla extract

55 g / 2 oz / ⅓ cup self-raising flour, sifted

2 tbsp mini marshmallows

**To decorate:**

30 g / 1 oz / ½ cup butter, softened

75 g / 2 ½ oz / ¾ cup icing (confectioners') sugar, plus extra for dusting

½ tsp vanilla extract

2–4 large marshmallow twirls

## Method

1. Beat the butter and sugar together in a mug until pale and creamy.

2. Break the egg into a second mug and add the vanilla extract. Beat gently with a fork, then gradually stir the egg into the butter mixture.

3. Fold in the flour and the mini marshmallows, then spoon half of the mixture into the mug you used to beat the egg and level the tops.

4. Transfer the mugs to a microwave and cook on full power for 1 ½ minutes. Test the cakes by inserting a skewer into the centre – if it comes out clean, they're ready. If not, return to the microwave for 15 seconds and test again. Leave the cakes to cool completely.

5. Beat the butter, icing sugar and vanilla extract together until pale and well whipped, adding a few drops of hot water if the mixture is too stiff.

6. Spoon the buttercream into a piping bag fitted with a large plain nozzle and pipe a big swirl on top of each cake.

7. Stick a marshmallow twirl into the top of each swirl and dust lightly with icing sugar.

# Banoffee Mug Cake

**Makes:** 1 | **Preparation Time:** 5 Minutes | **Cooking Time:** 1 ½ minutes

## Ingredients

30 g / 1 oz / ⅛ cup butter, softened

30 g / 1 oz / ⅛ cup caster (superfine) sugar

1 medium egg

30 g / 1 oz / ⅛ cup self-raising flour

1 tbsp milk

½ banana, mashed

**To decorate:**

½ banana, sliced

2 tbsp toffee sauce

## Method

1. Mix the butter and sugar in a large mug.

2. Add the egg and stir until well mixed.

3. Gradually stir in the flour, then add the milk and mix well.

4. Stir in the mashed banana.

5. Place the mug in the centre of the microwave and cook for 1 ½ minutes until well risen or until a skewer inserted in the centre comes out clean.

6. Decorate with slices of banana and drizzle with toffee sauce.

# Chocolate Espresso Mug Cake

**Makes:** 2 | **Preparation Time:** 30 minutes | **Cooking Time:** 1 ½ minutes

## Ingredients

55 g / 2 oz / ¼ cup butter, softened

55 g / 2 oz / ¼ cup caster (superfine) sugar

1 large egg

55 g / 2 oz / ⅓ cup self-raising flour, sifted

1 tsp instant espresso powder

1 tbsp cocoa powder

**To decorate:**

30 g / 1 oz / ½ cup butter, softened

75 g / 2 ½ oz / ¾ cup icing (confectioners') sugar

½ tsp instant espresso powder

cocoa powder for sprinkling

## Method

1. Beat the butter and sugar together in a mug until pale and smooth.

2. Break the egg into a second mug and beat gently with a fork, then gradually stir the egg into the butter mixture.

3. Fold in the flour, espresso powder and cocoa powder. Spoon half of the mixture into the mug you used to beat the egg and level the tops.

4. Transfer the mugs to a microwave and cook on full power for 1 ½ minutes. Test the cakes by inserting a skewer into the centre – if it comes out clean, the cakes are ready. If not, return to the microwave for 15 seconds and test again. Leave the cakes to cool completely.

5. Beat the butter, icing sugar and espresso powder together until pale and well whipped, adding a few drops of hot water if the mixture is too stiff.

6. Spoon or pipe the buttercream onto the cakes and dust with cocoa powder.

# Red Velvet Mug Cake

**Makes:** 1  |  **Preparation Time:** 10 Minutes  |  **Cooking Time:** 1 ½ minutes

## Ingredients

30 g / 1 oz / ⅛ cup butter, softened

30 g / 1 oz / ⅛ cup caster (superfine) sugar

1 medium egg

1 tbsp milk

1 tbsp red food dye

30 g / 1 oz / ⅛ cup self-raising flour

20 g / ¾ oz / ⅛ cup cocoa powder

**For the frosting:**

20 g / ¾ oz / ¼ cup cream cheese

20 g / ¾ oz / ¼ cup icing (confectioners') sugar

red sugar sprinkles

## Method

1. Mix the butter and sugar in a large mug.

2. Add the egg and stir until well mixed.

3. In a separate mug combine the milk and food dye.

4. Gradually stir in the flour and cocoa powder and add the milk; mix well.

5. Place the mug in the centre of the microwave and cook for 1 ½ minutes until the cake is well risen or a skewer inserted in the centre comes out clean.

6. To make the frosting, combine the cream cheese and icing sugar.

7. Top the cooled cake with the frosting and sugar sprinkles and serve.

# Gooey Chocolate Cream Mug Cake

**Makes:** 2 | **Preparation Time:** 30 Minutes | **Cooking Time:** 1 ½ minutes

## Ingredients

55 g / 2 oz / ¼ cup butter, softened

55 g / 2 oz / ¼ cup caster (superfine) sugar

1 large egg

55 g / 2 oz / ⅓ cup self-raising flour, sifted

2 tbsp cocoa powder

2 chocolate truffles

**To decorate:**

125 ml / 4 ½ fl. oz / ½ cup double (heavy) cream

cocoa powder for sprinkling

## Method

1. Beat the butter and sugar together in a mug until pale and smooth.

2. Break the egg into a second mug and beat gently with a fork, then gradually stir the egg into the butter mixture.

3. Fold in the flour and cocoa powder, then spoon half of the mixture into the mug you used to beat the egg. Press a chocolate truffle down into the centre of each cake and level the tops.

4. Transfer the mugs to a microwave and cook on full power for 1 ½ minutes or until the cake is well risen.

5. Leave the cakes to cool for 10 minutes while you prepare the cream. Whip the cream with an electric whisk until it holds its shape, then spoon it into a piping bag fitted with a large star nozzle.

6. Pipe a swirl of cream on top of each cake, then sprinkle with cocoa powder and serve immediately.

# Passion Fruit Mug Cake

**Makes:** 1  |  **Preparation Time:** 15 Minutes  |  **Cooking Time:** 2 Minutes

## Ingredients

30 g / 1 oz / ⅛ cup butter, softened

30 g / 1 oz / ⅛ cup caster
   (superfine) sugar

1 medium egg

30 g / 1 oz / ⅛ cup self-raising flour

1 tbsp milk

1 tbsp white chocolate chips

seeds and flesh of ½ passion fruit

### For the frosting:

20 g / ¾ oz / ¼ cup icing (confectioners')
   sugar

10 g / ⅓ oz / ⅛ cup soft butter

1 tbsp grated white chocolate

## Method

1.  Mix the butter and sugar in a large mug.

2.  Add the egg and stir until well mixed.

3.  Gradually stir in the flour, then add the milk and mix well.

4.  Stir in the chocolate chips and half of the passion fruit seeds.

5.  Place the mug in the centre of the microwave and cook for 1 ½ minutes until well risen or until a skewer inserted in the centre comes out clean. Allow to cool.

6.  To make the topping, combine the icing sugar and butter and mix until light and fluffy.

7.  Melt the white chocolate for 20 seconds in the microwave.

8.  Fold the melted white chocolate and remaining passion fruit into the frosting.

9.  Spoon the frosting onto the top of the cake and serve.

# Peanut Butter and Jam Mug Cake

---

**Makes:** 2 | **Preparation Time:** 30 minutes | **Cooking Time:** 1 ½ minutes

---

## Ingredients

55 g / 2 oz / ¼ cup butter, softened

55 g / 2 oz / ¼ cup caster (superfine) sugar

1 large egg

55 g / 2 oz / ⅓ cup self-raising flour, sifted

1 tbsp peanut butter

1 tbsp strawberry jam (jelly)

**To decorate:**

30 g / 1 oz / ½ cup butter, softened

75 g / 2 ½ oz / ¾ cup icing (confectioners') sugar, plus extra for dusting

2 tbsp peanut butter

1 tbsp strawberry jam (jelly)

## Method

1. Beat the butter and sugar together in a mug until pale and smooth.

2. Break the egg into a second mug and beat gently with a fork, then gradually stir the egg into the butter mixture.

3. Fold in the flour, followed by the peanut butter and jam, then spoon half of the mixture into the mug you used to beat the egg and level the tops.

4. Transfer the mugs to a microwave and cook on full power for 1 ½ minutes. Test the cakes by inserting a skewer into the centre – if it comes out clean, the cakes are ready. If not, return to the microwave for 15 seconds and test again. Leave the cakes to cool completely.

5. Beat the butter, icing sugar and peanut butter together until pale and well whipped.

6. Spoon the buttercream into a piping bag fitted with a large star nozzle and pipe a double ring round the edge of each cake.

7. Fill the centre of each buttercream ring with strawberry jam.

# Cinnamon Swirl Mug Cake

**Makes:** 1 | **Preparation Time:** 8 Minutes | **Cooking Time:** 4 Minutes

## Ingredients

30 g / 1 oz / ⅛ cup butter, softened

30 g / 1 oz / ⅛ cup caster
   (superfine) sugar

1 tsp ground cinnamon

1 medium egg

30 g / 1 oz / ⅛ cup self-raising flour

1 tbsp milk

**For the topping:**

1 tbsp caster (superfine) sugar

1 tsp boiling water

½ tsp ground cinnamon

20 g / ¾ oz / ¼ cup icing (confectioners')
   sugar

10 g / ⅓ oz / ⅛ cup soft butter

## Method

1. Mix the butter, sugar and cinnamon in a large mug.

2. Add the egg and stir until well mixed.

3. Gradually stir in the flour and add the milk; mix well.

4. Place the mug in the centre of the microwave and cook for 1 ½ minutes until well risen or until a skewer inserted in the centre comes out clean. Set aside.

5. In another mug, combine the caster sugar, water and cinnamon.

6. Cook in the microwave for 2 minutes and then allow to cool.

7. To make the frosting, combine the icing sugar and butter to make the buttercream.

8. Pipe or spoon the buttercream onto the cooled cake and then drizzle over the cinnamon syrup.

# Rocky Road Mug Cake

**Makes:** 2  |  **Preparation Time:** 35 minutes  |  **Cooking Time:** 1 ½ minutes

## Ingredients

55 g / 2 oz / ¼ cup butter, softened

55 g / 2 oz / ¼ cup caster (superfine) sugar

1 large egg

55 g / 2 oz / ⅓ cup self-raising flour, sifted

1 tbsp cocoa powder

1 tbsp dried cranberries

1 tbsp milk chocolate chunks

1 tbsp chopped mixed nuts

**To decorate:**

30 g / 1 oz / ½ cup butter, softened

75 g / 2 ½ oz / ¾ cup icing (confectioners') sugar, plus extra for dusting

1 tbsp cocoa powder

6 tbsp milk chocolate chunks

8 marshmallows

## Method

1.  Beat the butter and sugar together in a mug until pale and smooth.

2.  Break the egg into a second mug and beat gently with a fork, then gradually stir the egg into the butter mixture.

3.  Fold in the flour and cocoa powder, followed by the cranberries, chocolate chunks and nuts. Spoon half of the mixture into the mug you used to beat the egg and level the tops.

4.  Transfer the mugs to a microwave and cook on full power for 1 ½ minutes. Test the cakes by inserting a skewer into the centre – if it comes out clean, the cakes are ready. If not, return to the microwave for 15 seconds and test again. Leave the cakes to cool completely.

5.  Beat the butter, icing sugar and cocoa together until pale and well whipped, adding a few drops of hot water if the mixture is too stiff.

6.  Spoon the buttercream onto the cakes and top with 2 tbsp of the chocolate chunks and the marshmallows.

7.  Put the rest of the chocolate chunks in a mug. Melt in the microwave on medium in 5 second bursts until melted, stirring in between. Drizzle over the cakes and dust with icing sugar.

119

# Black Forest Mug Cake

Makes: 1  |  **Preparation Time:** 5 Minutes  |  **Cooking Time:** 1 ½ minutes

## Ingredients

40 g / 1 ½ oz / ¼ cup self-raising flour

40 g / 1 ½ oz / ¼ cup caster (superfine) sugar

20 g / ¾ oz / ⅛ cup cocoa powder

1 medium egg

2 tbsp milk

2 tbsp vegetable oil

1 tbsp chocolate chips

1 tbsp canned pitted black cherries

1 tbsp kirsch or cherry liqueur

## Method

1. Mix the flour, sugar and cocoa powder in a large mug.

2. Add the egg and thoroughly mix.

3. Combine the milk and oil in another mug, then add to the batter and stir.

4. Fold in the chocolate chips, cherries and liqueur.

5. Place the mug in the centre of the microwave and cook for 1 ½ minutes on full power.

6. Check the cake by placing a skewer into the centre of the cake, it should come out clean when fully cooked.

# Melt-in-the-middle Caramel Mug Cake

**Makes:** 2 | **Preparation Time:** 20 minutes | **Cooking Time:** 1 ½ minutes

## Ingredients

55 g / 2 oz / ¼ cup butter, softened

55 g / 2 oz / ¼ cup caster (superfine) sugar

1 large egg

55 g / 2 oz / ⅓ cup self-raising flour, sifted

1 ½ tbsp cocoa powder

6 squares caramel chocolate bar

## Method

1. Beat the butter and sugar together in a mug until pale and smooth.

2. Break the egg into a second mug and beat gently with a fork, then gradually stir the egg into the butter mixture.

3. Fold in the flour and cocoa powder, then spoon half of the mixture into the mug you used to beat the egg. Press 3 squares of the chocolate down into the centre of each cake and level the tops.

4. Transfer the mugs to a microwave and cook on full power for 1 ½ minutes or until well risen.

5. Leave the cakes to stand for 5 minutes before serving.

# White Chocolate and Raspberry Mug Cake

**Makes:** 1  |  **Preparation Time:** 5 Minutes  |  **Cooking Time:** 2 Minutes

## Ingredients

30 g / 1 oz / ⅛ cup butter, softened

30 g / 1 oz / ⅛ cup caster
  (superfine) sugar

1 medium egg

30 g / 1 oz / ⅛ cup self-raising flour

1 tbsp milk

1 tbsp white chocolate chips

1 tbsp freeze-dried raspberry pieces

**To decorate:**

1 tbsp white chocolate

fresh raspberries

## Method

1. Mix the butter and sugar in a large mug.

2. Add the egg and stir until well mixed.

3. Gradually stir in the flour, then add the milk
   and mix well.

4. Fold in the chocolate chips and the freeze-dried
   raspberry pieces.

5. Place the mug in the centre of the microwave
   and cook for 1 ½ minutes until well risen or until
   a skewer inserted in the centre comes out clean.

6. Melt the white chocolate for 20 seconds in
   the microwave.

7. Decorate with fresh raspberries and melted
   white chocolate.

# Index

**COCONUT, DESICCATED**
Coconut Lime Mug Cake, 73
Coconut Mug Cake, 16

**COFFEE AND CHICORY ESSENCE**
Café Latte Mug Cake, 95

**COFFEE ESSENCE**
Coffee and Walnut Mug Cake, 19

**COOKIES, CHOCOLATE**
Cookies and Cream Mug Cake, 96

**CRANBERRIES, DRIED**
Mini Fruit Mug Cake, 23
Orange and Cranberry Mug Cake, 62
Rocky Road Mug Cake, 119

**CREAM CHEESE**
Blackberry Cheesecake Mug Cake, 82
Carrot Mug Cake, 20
Red Velvet Mug Cake, 108

**CREAM, DOUBLE (HEAVY)**
Gooey Chocolate Cream Mug
  Cake, 111
Salted Caramel Mug Cake, 88
Sticky Toffee Mug Cake, 99

**CREAM OF TARTAR**
Strawberry Delight Mug Cake, 50

**CREAM, WHIPPING**
Blackberry Cheesecake Mug Cake, 82
Raspberry Pavlova Mug Cake, 65

**DATES**
Date and Walnut Mug Cake, 11
Sticky Toffee Mug Cake, 99

**ESPRESSO POWDER**
Chocolate Espresso Mug Cake, 107
Coffee and Walnut Mug Cake, 19
Nutty Coffee Mug Cake, 44

**FIGS, DRIED**
Pear and Fig Mug Cake, 78

**FOOD DYE**
Pistachio Mug Cake, 100
Red Velvet Mug Cake, 108

**FUDGE PIECES**
Vanilla Fudge Mug Cake, 92

**GINGER CONSERVE**
Ginger Mug Cake, 24

**GINGER, CRYSTALLISED**
Ginger Mug Cake, 24

**GINGER, GROUND**
Ginger Mug Cake, 24

**HAZELNUTS (COBNUTS)**
Mini Fruit Mug Cake, 23

**HONEY**
Honey and Lemon Mug Cake, 70

**ICE CREAM, COCONUT**
Coconut Mug Cake, 16

**JAM (JELLY), APRICOT**
Apricot Mug Cake, 81

**JAM (JELLY), RASPBERRY**
Raspberry Swirl Mug Cake, 74

**JAM (JELLY), STRAWBERRY**
Almond Mug Cake, 27
Peanut Butter and Jam Mug
  Cake, 115
Summer Fruit Mug Cake, 66
Victoria Sponge Mug Cake, 15

**KIRSCH**
Black Forest Mug Cake, 120

**LEMON**
Citrus Mug Cake, 58

Honey and Lemon Mug Cake, 70
Lemon Curd Mug Cake, 32
Lemon Drizzle Mug Cake, 40

**LEMON CURD**
Lemon Curd Mug Cake, 32

**LIME**
Citrus Mug Cake, 58
Coconut Lime Mug Cake, 73

**LIME EXTRACT**
Coconut Lime Mug Cake, 73

**MALTED CHOCOLATE BALLS**
Malted Chocolate Mug Cake, 91

**MAPLE SYRUP**
Maple and Pecan Mug Cake, 28

**MARMALADE**
Chocolate Chip Mug Cake, 39

**MARSHMALLOWS**
Marshmallow Surprise Mug Cake, 103
Rocky Road Mug Cake, 119

**MARZIPAN**
Marzipan Mug Cake, 36

**MERINGUES**
Raspberry Pavlova Mug Cake, 65

**MILK**
Almond Mug Cake, 27
Apple and Berry Mug Cake, 57
Banoffee Mug Cake, 104
Black Forest Mug Cake, 120
Carrot Mug Cake, 20
Cherry Mug Cake, 31
Chocolate Chip Mug Cake, 39
Chocolate Mug Cake, 12
Chocolate Orange Mug Cake, 53
Cinnamon Swirl Mug Cake, 116
Coconut Mug Cake, 16
Ginger Mug Cake, 24

Lemon Drizzle Mug Cake, 40
Orange and Cranberry Mug Cake, 62
Pistachio Mug Cake, 100
Raspberry Swirl Mug Cake, 74
Red Velvet Mug Cake, 108
Salted Caramel Mug Cake, 88
Summer Fruit Mug Cake, 66
Vanilla Fudge Mug Cake, 92
Victoria Sponge Mug Cake, 15
Passion Fruit Mug Cake, 112
White Chocolate and Raspberry Mug
    Cake, 124

**MIXED SPICE, GROUND**
Mini Fruit Mug Cake, 23

**NUTS, MIXED**
Rocky Road Mug Cake, 119

**ORANGE**
Chocolate Orange Mug Cake, 53
Orange and Cranberry Mug Cake, 62

**ORANGE EXTRACT**
Citrus Mug Cake, 58

**ORANGE LIQUEUR**
Orange and Cranberry Mug Cake, 62

**PASSION FRUIT**
Passion Fruit Mug Cake, 112

**PEANUT BUTTER**
Peanut Butter and Jam Mug
    Cake, 115

**PEAR**
Pear and Fig Mug Cake, 78

**PECAN NUTS**
Maple and Pecan Mug Cake, 28

**PINEAPPLE**
Pineapple and Banana Mug Cake, 69

**PISTACHIOS**
Mini Fruit Mug Cake, 23
Pistachio Mug Cake, 100

**RAISINS**
Cinnamon and Raisin Mug Cake, 43
Mini Fruit Mug Cake, 23

**RASPBERRIES**
Raspberry Pavlova Mug Cake, 65
White Chocolate and Raspberry Mug
    Cake, 124

**RASPBERRIES, FREEZE-DRIED**
Raspberry Swirl Mug Cake, 74
White Chocolate and Raspberry Mug
    Cake, 124

**SIROP DE FIGUE**
Pear and Fig Mug Cake, 78

**STRAWBERRIES**
Apple and Berry Mug Cake, 57
Strawberry Delight Mug Cake, 50
Victoria Sponge Mug Cake, 15

**SUGAR BALLS**
Citrus Mug Cake, 58

**SUGAR SPRINKLES**
Red Velvet Mug Cake, 108

**TOFFEE SAUCE**
Banoffee Mug Cake, 104

**VANILLA EXTRACT**
Apricot Mug Cake, 81
Banana Mug Cake, 47
Black Cherry Mug Cake, 77
Caffè Latte Mug Cake, 95
Cookies and Cream Mug Cake, 96
Date and Walnut Mug Cake, 11
Marshmallow Surprise Mug Cake, 103
Pineapple and Banana Mug Cake, 69
Salted Caramel Mug Cake, 88

Vanilla Fudge Mug Cake, 92
Vanilla Mug Cake, 8
Very Berry Mug Cake, 61
Victoria Sponge Mug Cake, 15

**VANILLA POD**
Vanilla Mug Cake, 8

**VEGETABLE OIL**
Black Forest Mug Cake, 120
Carrot Mug Cake, 20
Chocolate Mug Cake, 12
Chocolate Orange Mug Cake, 53

**WALNUTS**
Coffee and Walnut Mug Cake, 19
Date and Walnut Mug Cake, 11